A Robbie Reader

Gardening For Kids

A Kid's Guide to Landscape Design

Marylou Morano Kjelle

Mitchell Lane
PUBLISHERS

P.O. Box 196
Hockessin, Delaware 19707
Visit us on the web: www.mitchelllane.com
Comments? email us: mitchelllane@mitchelllane.com

Gardening For Kids

A Backyard Flower Garden for Kids

A Backyard Vegetable Garden for Kids

Design Your Own Butterfly Garden

Design Your Own Pond and Water Garden

A Kid's Guide to Landscape Design

A Kid's Guide to Perennial Gardens

Copyright © 2009 by Mitchell Lane Publishers

ABOUT THE AUTHOR: Marylou Morano Kjelle has written dozens of books for young readers. In addition to being a writer, she is a do-it-yourself gardener who is slowly landscaping all of the property surrounding her home in Central New Jersey. Each year Marylou plans and creates a new landscaping project. Some of the landscaping she has done includes planting small gardens alongside a wooden fence, planting flowering azalea bushes in front of her home, and creating container gardens around a backyard patio. Her gardens are a mix of annuals and perennials grown from seeds and bulbs. Marylou especially likes brightly colored flowers and blooming shrubs. Over the years, her landscaped backyard has become a place for her to rest, read, and write.

Printing 1 2 3 4 5 6 7 8 9

PUBLISHER'S NOTE: The facts on which the story in this book is based have been thoroughly researched. Documentation of such research can be found on page 45. While every possible effort has been made to ensure accuracy, the publisher will not assume liability for damages caused by inaccuracies in the data, and makes no warranty on the accuracy of the information contained herein.

Library of Congress Cataloging-in-Publication Data
Kjelle, Marylou Morano.
   A kid's guide to landscape design / by Marylou Morano Kjelle.
      p. cm. — (Robbie reader. Gardening for kids)
   Includes bibliographical references and index.
      ISBN 978-1-58415-637-6 (library bound)
      1. Landscape design—Juvenile literature.
I. Title. II. Series.
SB473.K568 2008
712—dc22
                                    2008002257

                                    PLB

Contents

Introduction

Landscaping—creating and designing a garden—is a fun way to learn about nature while making the place you live more beautiful. Landscaping is also a way for you to express your creativity. Landscaping a garden is a little like creating a piece of art. An interesting piece of sculpture or a lovely painting is something others admire and enjoy. Your piece of art—a beautiful garden—will be a thing of beauty you can be proud of.

Be sure to discuss your landscaping ideas with your parent or caregiver before you start your project. Let that person know what you are doing every step

of the way. If a landscaping project is too big for you to tackle alone, ask for help.

For landscape gardening, you'll want to keep a journal. It can be as simple as a scrapbook or a three-ring binder with pockets. Use it to record sunlight, soil conditions, and ideas. Fill it with photos, clippings, and sketches of things you want to try. You can record things you've tried that do or don't work.

Always garden safely and sensibly. Use gloves, knee protectors, bug spray, and even a mask if you have allergies. The sun is a friend to living things with petals, leaves, and stems, but it isn't as kind to humans. Always wear a hat and sunscreen to protect your skin from the sun's harmful rays.

Chapter

Chapter

1

Selecting a Space to Landscape

All artists begin the creative process with nothing more than an idea and a few tools. A sculptor begins with a lump of clay. A painter starts with a blank canvas. A landscaper begins with a plot of land that can be made more beautiful with colorful flowers, dramatic greenery, and interesting objects.

Part of the fun of creating a garden is deciding where to put it. Most people landscape their backyards and front yards, but patios, balconies, rooftops, and terraces can be landscaped as well. So can walkways, entranceways, and fences. Landscaping can make even the smallest and barest patch of ground more beautiful.

When checking out areas to landscape, you'll want to be sure the one you choose is a good place to grow a garden. Flowers, trees, and shrubs need certain growing conditions to survive. One very important growing condition is the climate, or usual weather conditions, and the **hardiness** zone. Most plants and shrubs are sold with a label that tells the zone in which they will thrive.

Any spot you choose to landscape must also have the right amount of sunlight and soil moisture, or wetness. Sunlight is the easier of the two to study, since it can be seen. Because the sun moves across the sky throughout the day, sunlight is weaker in the morning than it is in the afternoon. Different areas get sunshine at different times of the day. Some areas are sunny in the morning and shady in the afternoon. Others are shady in the morning but bright and sunny later in the day. Check the area you wish to landscape several times in one day. Look to see when, and for how long, it receives strong sunshine. Record this information in your gardening journal.

Garden Tip

Here's a test to help you determine if your soil is clay, sand, or loam. Do this test after it has rained, when the ground is damp but not soggy. Take a small amount of soil in your palms and try to form it into a ball about the size of a golf ball. Sandy soil can't be formed into a ball. Loam forms a ball that falls apart easily. Clay forms a ball that doesn't fall apart easily.

The information you collect about sunlight will help you decide which plants and flowers to grow in your space. Most flowering plants need about six hours of sunlight a day. The broadleaf purple coneflower, for example, needs direct sunlight; it won't grow well if it is planted in a shady area. Not all plants require direct sunlight. Flowers such as begonias prefer partial sunlight. They won't survive in an area that receives strong afternoon sunshine.

A nursery is a place where plants are raised and sold. Visiting a nursery will help you select the plants to place in your garden because you can see what they look like before you plant them.

Just because an area doesn't receive a lot of sun doesn't mean it isn't a good place for a garden. There are many plants that grow well in the shade. Impatiens is one of them.

Soil moisture is another growing condition that must be studied when choosing a space to landscape.

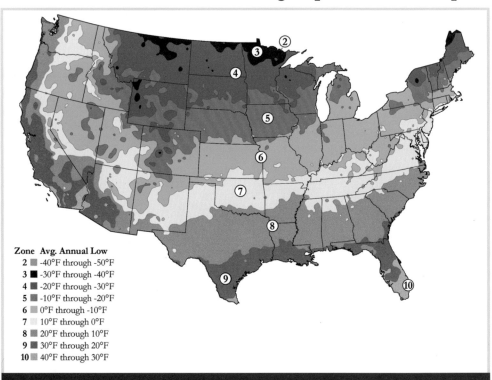

Zone Avg. Annual Low
2 -40°F through -50°F
3 -30°F through -40°F
4 -20°F through -30°F
5 -10°F through -20°F
6 0°F through -10°F
7 10°F through 0°F
8 20°F through 10°F
9 30°F through 20°F
10 40°F through 30°F

The United States is divided into hardiness zones. (Not pictured are Alaska, in Zone 1, and Hawaii, in Zone 11.) These zones are based on average winter temperature. Before choosing plants for your garden, you should know the hardiness zone of the area in which you live. Only choose plants that are known to grow well in your hardiness zone.

Pansies don't like heat, so they grow best in spring and early summer. Some types of pansies will even grow when snow is on the ground.

Purple coneflowers are great plants for attracting birds and butterflies to your garden. These flowers bloom all summer long.

Geraniums are easy-to-grow plants that will thrive in all types of climate conditions.

Begonias like partial shade. They bloom in many colors.

Certain types of plants won't grow in soil that is too wet or too dry. Soil contains spaces called pores. The number of pores affects how fast water drains from the soil. There are three basic types of soil. Sandy soil has a lot of pores, so water drains from it fast. Clay soil is very dense and has few pores; it holds water well. Loam contains sand and clay, as well as other materials. Water drains from loam at a rate that is good for most plants.

For the plants in your landscaped garden to be their healthiest, they must be matched with the right type of soil. Geraniums like moist soil. They may not grow if they are planted in soil that drains and dries out quickly. Sedum is a dry-soil plant. It won't grow well in soil that stays too moist. It does well in rock gardens.

Is the soil in your landscaped area sand, clay, or loam? Different plants grow best in different types of soil. Be sure you know which type of soil you have before you begin planting.

Sedum grows well in rock gardens. With more than 600 varieties of sedum from which to choose, there's sure to be a type that is just right for your landscaped area.

Sunlight and soil moisture are two important things to consider when landscaping a garden. Studying how much of each an area gets will help you choose the best space to landscape and the type of plants you will use. Deciding on a space is just the first step in the landscaping process. Once you have your space, it's time to create a design.

13

Chapter 2

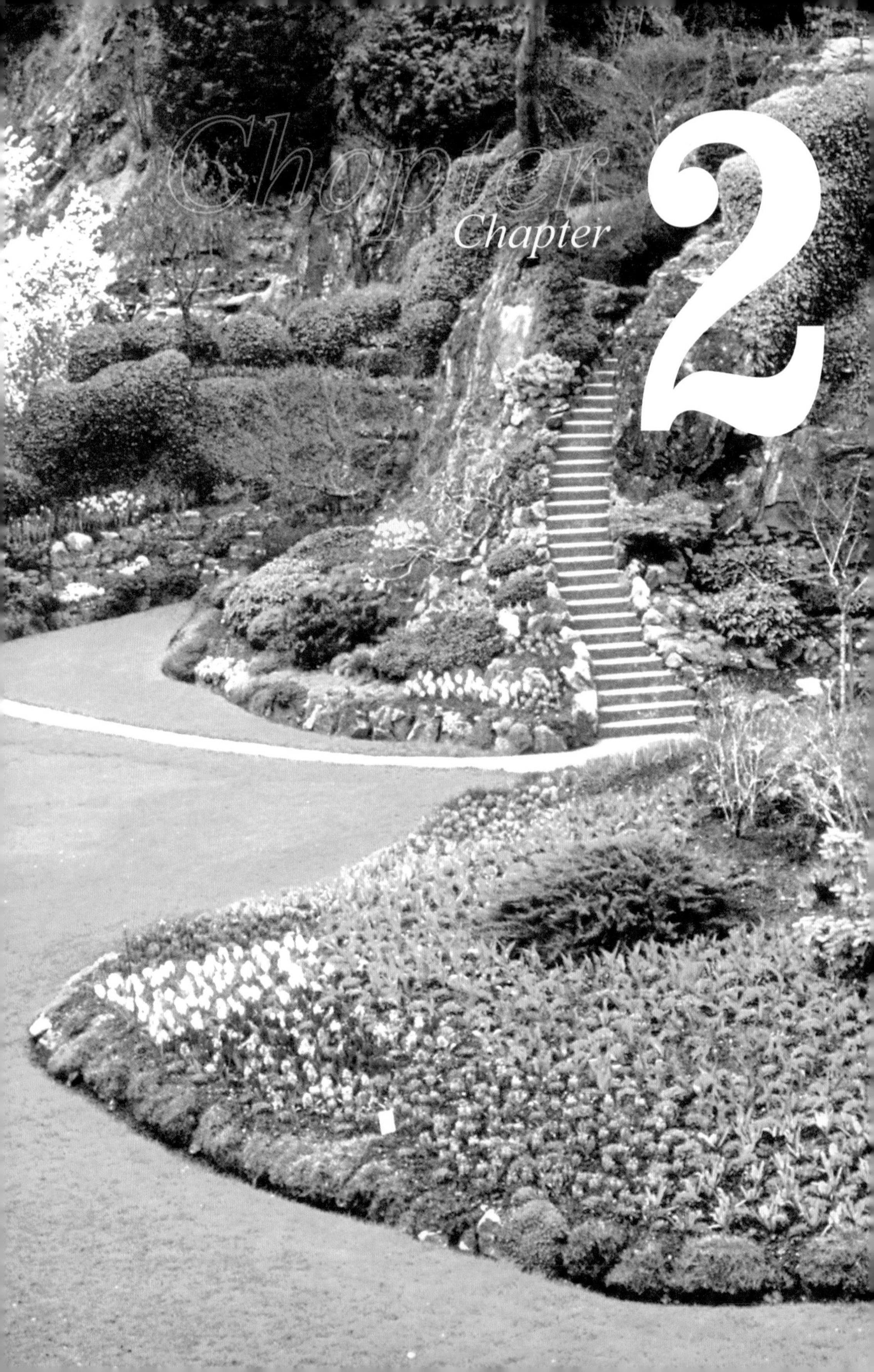

Creating a Landscape Design

Professional landscapers use photography to help them design a landscape. They photograph the area they have selected from several different angles and then study the pictures. You should photograph the space you wish to landscape, and paste the pictures in your garden journal. You can refer to them as you create your landscape design.

The photographs will show you what the space looks like before you start your landscape project. For example, what is in or around the space? Are there trees and plants? Will they be part of your garden, or will they have to be cleared away? If there are trees nearby, do they block the sunlight? Is there a house, garage, or other building near the area you have selected? If so, how will it fit into your landscape design?

Decide whether you want your garden to fit into the surrounding area or stand alone. Then, using your photographs, make a rough sketch of the area you have in mind. Use graph paper to draw your sketch to scale. For example, if the space you are planning to landscape is six feet long and three feet wide, draw your sketch so that two blocks on the graph paper equal one foot of the garden. Your drawing will be twelve blocks long and six blocks wide. If you like working on the computer, you can find software that will help you make design drawings.

First sketch the garden's border. A border will add interest as well as define your garden. A straight border is fine if you are landscaping along the side of a house or a fence. If your garden will be in the middle of a yard, an unusual shape will make it more interesting.

Garden Tip

Even the most carefully tended garden will sprout a weed or two once in a while. If left in the flower bed, weeds will rob the plants of food and nutrients and eventually cause them to die. Protect your flowers and plants by weeding your garden once a week while it is in full bloom. Be sure you remove the entire weed, including the root. A small handheld shovel or trowel will help you do the job.

A garden can be landscaped within an oval, circle, triangle, or even an irregular shape. How about landscaping several smaller areas within a larger yard? Be sure the area you choose is not used for playing, cooking, entertaining, or pets.

Your sketch should show the area surrounding your bordered garden. Include nearby buildings, such as houses, garages, or sheds. Also place walkways and driveways in your drawing. Next sketch the shrubs, trees, and plants that are already within your bordered area that you plan to keep. Whatever space

A good landscaper plans before beginning to work in the soil. Sketch your ideas in your gardening journal before you start working in the garden, and look at your drawing often as you landscape your area.

is left within the border is the area you will landscape.

Borders can be made of wood, stone, metal, or plastic. Bricks are often used to create borders because they can be arranged in many ways. For example, they can be lined up side by side or set in a zigzag pattern. They can be placed into the soil on their sides, or they can be stacked on one another.

Other materials that make good borders are stones, wood, flagstone, shells, and old railroad ties. Border material made from a variety of substances can be found in your local gardening store. Colorful plants that grow close to the ground can become a living border.

Let your imagination run wild when planning a border for your landscaped area. Shells, rocks, bricks and many other items make interesting borders for gardens.

A focal point
like this bird-
bath makes a
landscaped
area interesting.
Plus it's great
for bird-
watching!

19

Once you have defined your space by sketching a border, decide on the garden's focal point. A focal point is an object—either living or nonliving—that draws attention to the garden. The focal point will be the first thing someone sees when they look at your garden. Draw your focal point in your sketch. A ceramic animal, garden statue, attractive piece of driftwood, birdhouse, or birdbath are all objects that make good focal points. Shrubs, bushes, or small trees can be living focal points.

Gardening magazines and books have pictures of different landscape designs. Studying these pictures will give you ideas for your own landscaped area.

Large elements like a bench or a trellis help make a landscaped area a welcoming place to rest and relax.

Next, include in your sketch anything that you want to put in your garden. If your garden will be created alongside a fence, you can incorporate the fence into your landscape design with climbing plants like sweet pea and morning glory. These will climb up and over a fence, covering it with leaves and flowers. A trellis can serve as a focal point, and also hide things that might take away from the beauty of a garden, such as a wall or an air-conditioning unit.

Landscaping ideas are everywhere. You can find designs for a garden by reading books, visiting a local nursery, or seeing how your neighbors have landscaped their gardens.

Chapter

3

Pulling It All Together

You've chosen your area to landscape, and you have made a rough sketch that includes a border, a focal point, and any existing elements that will remain. The next step is to decide on the plants, shrubs, and other objects that you will use.

The pieces of a landscape design—its living and nonliving elements—must all look like they belong together. One of the ways to make this happen is to create a design that has balance. Balance will depend on the landscaped area's size and shape. Larger pieces, such as taller and fuller shrubs and bushes, should be placed toward the back of a garden. Smaller plants should go in front of them. This type of design works well in circular spaces. Or you can try to achieve symmetry (SIH-muh-tree) by having one end of your garden mirror the other end. Whatever is placed on the left side of the garden is also placed on the right side. This is a popular landscaping technique for square or rectangular gardens.

Flowers and small plants will add color to your design. If you want your garden to have a warm effect, choose red, pink, and orange flowers. Purple and blue flowers give a cooler effect. Planting flowers around the existing trees and shrubs adds new growth to old and makes all the living things look like they belong together.

You can check out flower color by looking at gardening books or by going online. You'll see that there is no limit to the color variations from which to choose. Lighter flower colors open up a space and make it look larger. They brighten a shady spot. Darker flowers add drama when they are mixed with silvery plants. You may decide to design a garden that contains flowers that are all one color. You may mix colors for dramatic effect.

Keep in mind the area's sunlight, soil moisture, and hardiness zone when selecting the living elements of your area. For your garden to grow and thrive, you

When looking through magazines and gardening catalogs, note the colors of the flowers, as well as their size. If you like something, cut out the picture (ask permission first) and keep it in a file or paste it into your journal.

In addition to making a garden look pretty, flowers make a garden smell pretty. Their smell attracts bees and other insects. As an insect flies from flower to flower, it spreads pollen, which allows the plant to make seeds.

25

must match the plant to the growing conditions.

Strive for a balance of size and color as you plan your landscape design. You already have a sketch of your border, focal point, and existing elements. Now sketch out a few possible designs that add the other elements. Sketch in the largest elements first, and fill in with smaller flowers and plants as you go along. Use colored pencils to see how the flower colors work together. You are working with living things that will grow over time, so don't overcrowd your garden. You can always fill in bare spots after it has been growing for a while.

Landscapers usually plan in the winter months, when it's too cold to work outside. Once there is no longer a danger of frost, they begin to work. The border will define your design, so it should be the first thing you install. A garden hose can help. Following the design of your sketch, position the garden hose until it is in the shape of your border. Then use chalk to trace the hose's outline. Shovel a shallow trench along the inside of the line, keeping the soil you remove. If you will be using nonliving

Garden Tip

You may want to consider a plant's smell when planning your garden. Jasmine is often used to make perfume. It smells the best in the morning, around sunrise. Lavender has a sweet smell. The flower most often selected for its smell is the rose.

A shallow trench will help you establish the boundary for your landscaped area. Rocks, shells, and other materials can then be placed into the trench to form a border.

It's easy to make your own compost. All you need is a sunny patch of lawn and organic matter. Spring is the best time to start composting. Place grass clippings and shredded leaves in a pile. Add food scraps from the kitchen. These can include eggshells, fruit and vegetable peels, coffee grounds, and tea bags. (Do not include meat scraps.) Some people keep a small plastic bucket in the kitchen to collect these things. Turn your compost pile over with a shovel or pitchfork at least once a week. Keep the pile moist.

Compost is produced when earthworms, bacteria, and insects break down the organic matter. Within a short time, a rich, dark material will form on the bottom of the pile. Shovel it up and spread it over your flower beds. From garbage has come food—food for plants!

material for your border, such as stone or brick, place it in the trench. Be sure it is embedded firmly in the ground. If your garden will have a living border of flowers, plant them last.

Next prepare the **bed**, or planting area. First remove everything from the site that you do not want in your garden. This includes old plants and shrubs, weeds, large rocks, and other objects. Then use a pitchfork to turn over the soil within the border until it has all been loosened. Work from the border toward the center of your design.

This is a great time to add **nutrients** (NOO-tree-entz). **Compost** is a mixture of decaying **organic** matter (like leaves, grass clippings, and vegetable scraps from the kitchen). Work this mixture into the loosened soil. Then use a rake to **grade** the bed by spreading the soil and compost mixture evenly and smoothly over the surface of the garden.

Once the ground is ready, add any nonliving structures you want in your garden, such as a birdbath, bench, statue, or trellis. Now comes the really fun part. Let's get planting!

Caring for Your Landscape

The best time to plant flowers and young shrubs and bushes is late spring and early summer. By then the danger of frost has passed. Planting at this time will give the roots of the plants enough time to firmly attach to the soil before the heat of the summer.

There's a lot to consider when choosing plants and flowers for your garden. Some plants live for only one season and then die. They are called **annuals**, and they need to be replanted each year. Annuals bloom from late spring to early fall. Impatiens, marigolds, and petunias are popular annuals.

Perennials are plants that live for more than two years. They will bloom each year without replanting. Tulips, hyacinths, and daffodils are perennials that bloom in the early spring. Another perennial, chrysanthemums (also called mums), bloom in late summer and early fall. Many perennials are planted as bulbs at different times of the year, depending on when they bloom. A landscaped garden that includes a mixture of perennials and annuals is always in bloom.

Plants can be put in the ground in three ways: as seeds, as bulbs, or as young plants. Starting

plants from seeds will not only save you money, it will let you watch your plant grow from the very beginning. Seeds usually come in packets, and they can be purchased at any home and garden store. To start the seeds indoors, you will need small pots or containers for planting (egg cartons work well), potting soil (also available at a home and garden store), labels, plastic wrap, and water. Start the seeds in late spring, or about six weeks before you are ready to plant them in the garden.

Check the seed packet for any special growing instructions. If there are none, follow these steps. Loosely fill the containers almost to the top with potting soil. Don't pack it in. Gently sprinkle the seeds onto the soil. Cover them with more potting soil and press down very gently. Water the soil lightly and cover it loosely with plastic wrap. Put the containers with the seeds in a warm, dry place. Check each day for signs of growth. Water lightly when needed. Once sprouts appear, remove the plastic and move the containers to a slightly sunny location. Keep the soil moist. As the seeds grow into plants, place

Always read the back of the seed packet before planting. It will tell you important information about the plant and its growing conditions.

the containers in direct sunlight. Once leaves are visible, gently move each seedling to a larger pot. Plant the seedlings in the ground once there is no longer a danger of frost.

Seeds can also be planted directly in the ground, and then covered with a light layer of soil.

Bulbs should be planted in a hole that is three times as deep as the bulb is long. For example, if the bulb is two inches long, the hole it is planted in should be six inches deep. Hyacinths, daffodils, and tulips

Whether you are planting seeds, bulbs, or starter plants, using the proper planting tools and supplies will make landscaping easier and result in a more beautiful garden.

When you begin to plant, follow the sketch that you made in your gardening journal. It will tell you exactly where each plant should go.

should be buried with the point of the bulb facing upward. Plant these bulbs in the fall for spring blooms.

The fastest way to bring structure and color to your garden is by buying young plants and placing them directly into the soil. Look for plants whose roots aren't crowded, and put the plants in the ground as soon as you have purchased them. Annuals and perennials are often sold in flats—a tray of 20 small plants. Remove each plant from the tray and place it in a hole that is a little wider and deeper than the plant's **root-ball.** Always water plants as soon as they have been planted.

After they are in the ground, flowers continue to need care. Watch for signs of **dehydration** (dee-hy-DRAY-shun). If rainfall is scarce, use a garden hose or watering can to water them.

Feed the plants with a ready-made mix about once a month during the growing season. You can buy this at a garden center. Follow the instructions. Using plant food will help new flowers to grow. Another way to encourage flower growth is by **deadheading**, or removing dead flowers. You can use your fingernails or small scissors to pinch off the dead blossoms. This prevents the plant from producing seeds. Instead the plant's energy is used to create more flowers.

Once all of your plants are in the ground, you should add **mulch** to your garden. Wood chips make

Small starter plants can be planted directly in the ground. Covering the flower bed with mulch after you have planted will help the soil stay wet and stop weeds from growing.

good mulch. Spread a thin, even layer of chips over the ground around your plants. Mulch will help keep moisture in the soil, and it will slow the growth of weeds. It will make your garden look tidy, too.

The height of plants gives a landscaped area its structure. Not all plants are meant to be tall. One way to control plant height is to pinch back new growth above a joint. This will cause a plant to become fuller rather than taller.

Check on your plants often during the growing season. Water, feed, deadhead, mulch, and pinch as often as needed. Your garden will reward your attention with healthy plants and beautiful color.

Chapter **5**

Creative Landscape Ideas

Once you have mastered the landscape basics of structure, balance, and color, you can use them to create any type of garden.

A rock garden is an interesting way to put your landscaping skills to work. When planning this type of garden, look for an area with good drainage. You'll need rocks of various sizes and shapes. They can be purchased at a garden store or dug up from the surrounding area. Group a few smaller rocks in various positions before placing them permanently in the garden. Keep changing the arrangement until you like the way it looks. Place the rocks so that they are firmly in the ground. Aim for a natural look.

A small fountain or waterfall adds a nice touch to a garden. The sound of gently running water is soothing, and it will attract people to your landscaped area. A pump moves the water through the fountain or waterfall. The pump will need electricity, so keep that in mind before you choose a location. You will need an adult's permission and help to install a water system.

Another fun garden to plan is a themed garden. For a patriotic theme, use plants whose flowers are red, white, and blue. Insert small flags into your landscape design to complete the patriotic look.

You can also create a bird-friendly garden. Purple coneflowers, snapdragons, and sunflowers will attract birds to your garden. Install a birdhouse nearby—but don't put it too close to the garden. When birds are raising their young, they don't like people to get near the house. You won't be able to care for your garden every day without making them nervous. Don't forget to include a birdbath in your bird-themed landscape.

A fountain makes a good focal point for a landscaped area, while rocks of all sizes add color and texture.

What does an old shoe have in common with a teapot? A rusty pail with a discarded rubber tire? All of these objects can become small-scale landscapes when used as containers for plants. The roots of plants

Watching a plant grow from seed to flower is a great way to study nature and connect with living things.

can't spread out as much in a container as they can in the soil. Plants in containers will have a hard time getting water and nutrients. You'll need to pay extra attention to the watering and feeding of container gardens.

Container gardens can be moved around, so their location can be changed every few weeks. Filled with multicolored flowers and eye-catching green plants, they will make even the most unattractive corner come to life.

Just as a piece of art tells us a lot about the artist, a nicely landscaped garden tells us about the person who designed and planted it. You chose an area for your garden and drew up a design. You selected a focal point, planted flowers and shrubs, and installed a border around your garden. From your "blank canvas," a beautiful garden has emerged.

The garden you have created is a thing of beauty, a work of art. It's an interesting place to enjoy nature and sit and rest awhile. While you may think you have come to the end of your landscaping project, you have really only begun. Landscape projects evolve. This means they change over time. When the next

Garden Tip

Take photographs of your garden throughout the growing season. You took pictures of the area when it was still untouched in order to plan your design. You should also take photos after you put in seedlings and new shrubs.

Put your garden photos in order and paste them into your gardening journal. Watching your garden "grow" in photos is a lot of fun! It's also a great way to remember what you planted.

growing season comes around, you may want to add new plants to your landscape design. Or you may decide to start landscaping another area. Either way, you will have created a landscape garden that you can enjoy for many years to come.

 **Craft**

Make Your Own Seed Markers

You Will Need
Wooden spoons (available at a craft store)
Waterproof markers
Empty seed packets
Glue
Spray-on varnish (available at a home improvement store)
Old newspapers

1. Cut out the picture on the seed packet.
2. Glue the picture onto a wooden spoon.
3. On the other side of the spoon, use a waterproof marker to write the name of the plant.
4. After the glue is dry, **ask an adult** to help you spray varnish onto both sides of the spoon. You may need more than one coat. Let the varnish dry between coats.

5. Place the spoons in the ground where your seeds are planted to mark their space and remind you of what the flowers will look like.

Further Reading

Books

Krezel, Cindy, and Bruce Curtis. *Kids' Container Gardening: Year-Round Projects for Inside and Out.* Batavia, Illinois: Ball Publishing, 2005.

Matthews, Clare, and Clive Nichols. *Great Gardens for Kids.* London: Hamlyn, 2005.

———. *How Does Your Garden Grow?: Great Gardening for Green-Fingered Kids.* London: Hamlyn, 2005.

Rushing, Felder. *Dig, Plant, Grow: A Kid's Guide to Gardening.* Nashville, Tennessee: Cool Springs Press, 2003.

Works Consulted

Bartlett Tree Research Laboratories: Soil Drainage
   http://www.bartlett.com/sv420.cfm#top

Corlett, Keith. *Garden Design for Small Spaces.* New York: Sterling Publishing Company, Inc., 2004.

Edwards, Jonathan. *How to Garden.* New York: Hermes House, 2002.

Gardening Landscaping and Design
   http://www.hgtv.com/hgtv/gl_landscaping_design/

Holmes, Roger, and Rita Buchanan. *Mid-Atlantic Home Landscaping.* Upper Saddle River, New Jersey: Creative Homeowner, 2006.

The Landscape Design Site
   http://www.the-landscape-design-site.com/

Murray, Elizabeth, and Derek Fell. *Home Landscaping.* New York: Simon & Schuster, 1988.

Peel, Lucy. *Family Garden: A Practical Guide to Creating a Fun and Safe Family Garden.* Hauppauge, New York: Barron's Educational Services, 1999.

Further Reading

Simonds, John Ormsbee. *Landscape Architecture*. Third Edition. New York: McGraw Hill, 1998.

Swenson, Allan A. *The Everything Landscaping Book*. Avon, Massachusetts: Adams Media Corporation, 2003.

United States National Arboretum
http://www.usna.usda.gov/

On the Internet

Gardening for Kids
http://www.geocities.com/EnchantedForest/Glade/3313/

Junior Master Gardener
http://www.jmgkids.us/

University of Illinois Extension: My First Garden
http://www.urbanext.uiuc.edu/firstgarden/planning/index.html

Glossary

annuals (AN-yoo-ulz)—Plants grown from seeds that die in one year.

bed (BED)—The plot of land in which plants are rooted.

compost (KOM-pohst)—A mixture of broken-down organic matter used to enrich the soil with nutrients.

dehydration (dee-hy-DRAY-shun)—Loss of moisture.

feed (FEED)—To fertilize a plant or plants.

grade (GRAYD)—To even out a patch of soil for planting.

deadheading (DED-hed-ing)—Removing dead flowers from a living plant.

hardiness (HAR-dee-nes)—The amount of cold a plant is able to withstand.

mulch (MULCH)—A covering of wood chips or other matter that helps plants retain moisture and discourages weed growth.

nutrients (NOO-tree-entz)—Substances that help things grow.

organic (or-GAA-nik)—Made from parts of plants or animals.

perennials (pur-EN-ee-alz)—Plants that live longer than two years.

root-ball (ROOT-ball)—A plant's tangle of roots.

symmetry (SIH-muh-tree)—Having balance, looking the same on two sides.

Index